ARE YOU
—— THE ——
CHRIST?

Finding the Goodness in Yourself & Others

K. Morgan deCasenave Patterson

Parker House Publishing
ParkerHouseBooks.com

Front cover quote from online dictionary.
Hafiz translations are from the Penguin publication *The Gift:
Poems by Hafiz*, by Daniel Ladinsky. Copyright © 1999 Daniel
Ladinsky and used with his permission.

Jelaluddin Rumi, poem *The Guest House* translation by Coleman
Barks, used with his permission.

Bible verse: Matthew 25: verses 34–40, World English Bible

Editing: AroundTheWritersTable.com
Cover design: JCH Design, LLC
Production: Parker House Publishing

ISBN: 978-0692551097

What people are saying...

Morgan Patterson has written a wonderful and very thought-provoking book entitled *Are you the Christ?* When I first started to read the book and title, I was honestly turned off as I was brought up Jewish and probably relate more to Buddhism now than anything else. However, for some very unknown reason I went back and read the book and was so impressed.

What Morgan has done remarkably well in this book is to show us that we all have a god-like quality embedded in us and the secret of life is to see this in others as well as ourselves. Morgan shows us from her vantage point of how she does this, and we all can learn so much from her beautifully written stories of the Christ she now sees wherever she looks.

We all can learn so much from Morgan's teachings.

~ Jerry Osteryoung, Ph.D.
Professor Emeritus at Florida State
University, Author of 8 books

~~~~~~

The essays in *Are You the Christ?* coupled with Hafiz's poetry provide an opportunity to connect with a deep truth within us all.

The delicious nuggets in this book will cause you to think, to examine and to consider your reality in a new and expansive way. You'll never see other people, or yourself, in the same way again.

Thank you, Morgan, for reminding me to be ever present to "the One" in all of us.

~ Trish Carr, Speaker, Coach,
Bestselling Author

~~~~~~

Thank you for this beautiful piece of work which inspires us to see people beyond our own veils of judgment and preconceived notions. Your book creates the opportunity for us to experience humanity and this journey we call life with a renewed sense of understanding, compassion, and love. This is a book for everyone to read!

~ Nancy Matthews, Speaker,
Author, Global Leader

Dedication

This book is dedicated to all those I have met and will meet that require me to look deeply at myself and others.

To my family: my husband Gregg; my kids Sean, Candace, Jessica and Pat; my grandchildren Tyler, Sophia, Lyric, Layla, Jillian, Shepherd, Tess, and Jared; and my mother who loved me no matter what—you all encourage me daily to recognize that we, too, are the Christ!

Acknowledgements

Much gratitude to all those who have assisted in the creation of this book... Daniel Ladinsky and his agent Nancy Barton, who has spent hours helping me get this to print; Coleman Barks for his generosity; Gina Edwards and her amazing editing along with holding my hand and encouraging me; Candi Parker at ParkerHouseBooks.com for never becoming tired of my many changes; the amazing book cover by James Hamer at JCH Designs, he has an amazing ability to really hear and feel what I was truly trying to portray; Gail Dixon, Nancy Matthews, Jerry Osteryoung and Trish Carr for their willingness to take the time to read this book and their generous words which so touched my heart, bringing tears to my eyes; Licia Berry a true healer and great friend, who continues to play such a huge part in my private and professional life, aiding in the healing necessary to see this work to completion.

Thank you to all; you have encouraged and supported me during this creation!

FOREWORD

I was grateful to be asked to write the foreword for this book; I'm so moved by it.

I've known Morgan deCasenave Patterson since she came to a reading of my 2012 memoir *SOUL COMPOST – Transforming Adversity into Spiritual Growth*. I was touched by her sight, her ability to be fully present and open to the goodness in all people.

When we don't recognize the Christ in ourselves, we harm one another.... we create an un-Christ-like world. Without a model to teach us to love ourselves and recognize our Christ-like nature, we forget that love is the answer, always. When we recognize the goodness inside of ourselves, we are also able to recognize the goodness in others. We accept others as flawed just as we are, just as Jesus recognized the good in others and loved and accepted them anyway. Where did we forget this essential message?

When the man Yeshua ben Joseph (also known as the Christ) came into the world, the Roman Empire was in full swing. The Romans took no prisoners and consumed and destroyed and enslaved and dominated; it was a precarious time to be in the world and dangerous to good people who tried to just live their lives in peace. The love of Christ is what the world needed, and the Universe provided the answer to the need. With a heart aflame, he was a man, a flesh and blood human being, inspired with a vision of how the world could be. He had emotion and a body, a mind and spirit, just like us. His story is not unlike the stories of many of us who have a vision of a better world, but meet opposition from ingrained behavior and thought. Many of us are 'crucified' by others' words, actions, and thoughts.

I, for one, feel the sacredness inherent in a person who is called to challenge the cultural norms, whether they be a biker, a writer, a healer, a teller of truth. God works in mysterious ways, and I can think of nothing more mysterious than how we got to this place in the world of environmental catastrophe, rampant racism, sexism, homophobia, and terrorism. Perhaps it is because we have a choice and we can change it if we want to. The change-makers are the courageous souls who, like Jesus, seek to create heaven on earth, a place of acceptance, peace, and love. All those who challenge injustice and inequality are, by definition, Christ-like.

Morgan deCasenave Patterson has done just this in writing this illuminating book; she has challenged our idea that only the "special" or "the revered" can identify as the Christ. Love comes in many packages, and often in the most humble, quiet, and unassuming. As she correctly points out, the spirit of Jesus walks among us as an equal, within each of us. Will we see the holiness right in front of us? Will we see the holiness inside our own hearts?

The potential for humanity to create heaven on Earth lies within our choice to awaken from the societal sleep. We may not recognize that our fervent desire to "be saved" is rooted in our cultural conditioning that we are unworthy, less than divine. Like the author, I challenge this belief system, and call upon you and all of us to lovingly, gently open the door to another possibility . . . that we are all the Christ within.

Licia Berry
Author, Artist, Shamana, July 2015

Essays by K. Morgan deCasenave Patterson

ARE YOU THE CHRIST?

Poems by Hafiz: Translated by Daniel Ladinsky

AND THEN YOU ARE
TODAY
BETWEEN YOUR EYE AND THIS PAGE
HOW DO I LISTEN
STAY WITH US
ONLY ONE RULE
NOW IS THE TIME
YOU'RE IT
ALL THE TALENTS OF GOD
WHAT IS THE ROOT

Poem by Rumi: Translated by Coleman Barks

THE GUEST HOUSE

Table of Contents

INTRODUCTION

When the title of this book, *Are You the Christ*, first came to me, I was sitting at home minding my own business. At first, I wasn't sure what it meant.

I usually consider myself a fairly non-judgmental person. Mostly, I believe in letting people be who and what they are—at least that's what I thought about myself. But, that day, it became incredibly obvious to me that this was not the truth I was living. I believe it is the truth of who we all are, deep down, but in my day-to-day life, that was not how I was showing up.

We live our daily lives, wandering the streets, passing each other by. We walk past thousands upon thousands of people in our lifetimes. Who are they? Who are they REALLY? The next thing I knew, the plan for what this book should be revealed itself, like images in a three-D movie.

Introduction

Do you ever ask yourself these questions? Who are all these people and do they really matter in my day-to-day life? Today, are they the least bit important for my tomorrow? Must I respond to them as if they matter or can I continue to walk, never knowing who they are?

This book is about all those people we see and just as quickly judge. It is about what happens when we stop and take a really good look. Even though they wear pants hanging so low they must hold the front to keep them up, even though they have tattoos and piercings all over their bodies, even though they holler at people as they drive by, even though they look or act differently from us, they might be the one who will change our day, maybe even change our lives. You know, they just might be the Christ.

How will you know? How will you be able to tell if this person is the Christ? You may have to take the time to slow down and be with them, bring yourself to be the presence, and to be present with each and every one you come in contact with. This might cramp your style. This may slow down your day. But what if—just what if—that person you just passed, without even making eye contact, is the Christ? What if you ignored the person who will save your life? Can you stop and find the good within each of those you meet, and thus, in yourself as well?

This book, I hope will challenge you to look at yourself with a very different eye, and as importantly, to look at those you pass with the same compassion as those you love. Can you see and—as written in many sacred texts— recognize and remember that what we do to the least of the children, we do to the Christ?

— *K. Morgan deCasenave Patterson*

Introduction

୭

"Then the King will tell those on his right hand, 'Come, blessed of my Father, inherit the Kingdom prepared for you for the foundation of the world; for I was hungry, and you gave me food to eat. I was thirsty, and you gave me drink. I was a stranger, and you took me in. I was naked, and you clothed me. I was sick, and you visited me. I was in prison, and you came to me.'

"Then the righteous will answer him, saying, 'Lord, when did we see you hungry, and feed you; or thirsty, and give you a drink? When did we see you as a stranger, and take you in; or naked, and clothe you? When did we see you sick, or in prison, and come to you?'

"The King will answer them, 'Most certainly I tell you, because you did it to one of the least of these my brothers, you did it to me.'"

୭

AND THEN YOU ARE

And then You are like this:

A small bird decorated
With orange patches of light
Waving Your wings near the window,

Encouraging me with all of existence's love—
To dance.

And then You are like this:

A cruel word that stabs me
From the mouth of a strange costume You
wear;
A guise You had too long tricked me into
thinking
Could be other—than You.

And then You are...

The firmament
That spins at the end of a string in Your hand
That You offer to mine saying,
"Did you drop this—surely
This is yours."

K. Morgan deCasenave Patterson | 5

And then You are, O then You are;

The Beloved of every creature
Revealed with such grandeur—bursting
From each cell in my body,
I kneel, I laugh,
I weep, I sing,
I sing.

—*Hafiz (tr. Ladinsky)*

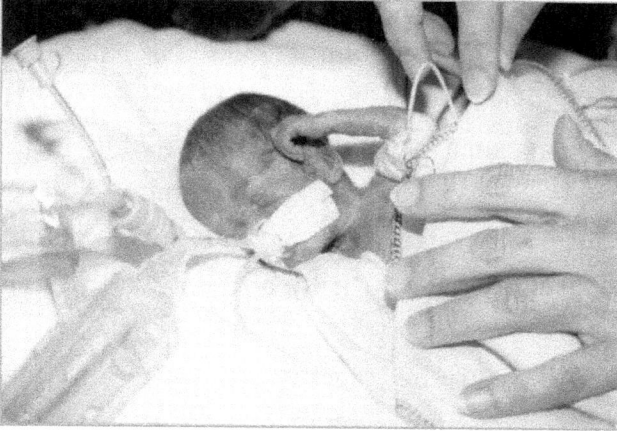

Are You the Christ?

I sit looking at you, tiny creature, knowing that you have had only twenty-three weeks inside your safe and protective environment. Most infants get to be nurtured the full forty. You keep your eyes closed as if you just aren't ready to see this new world. I see directly into your body—the blood flowing, your heart beating. You could and should still be cradled inside your mother, protected from the sights, sounds, and presence of this harsh outside world.

Are You the Christ?

As I watch you grow and become a teenager, you remind me on a regular basis that, oh yes, you are certainly the Christ. You walk in such a way that your divinity shines brightly, even in the darkest moments. You continually remind me and those around you of what and who you truly are—of who *we* truly are.

Are you the Christ? The question never crossed my mind when you were an infant. Will you survive? Will you be healthy? Will I see you grow up? Yes, those were the questions in the forefront of my thoughts. But never, are you the Christ?

Now, the words of Hafiz bring this question to the forefront, when he says, "A strange costume You wear; a guise You had too long tricked me into thinking could be other than You."

How many times, how often do I miss You? You, the Christ, because in my life, and in the world "You have tricked me into thinking there could be any other than You"?

Ah, yes. You are the Christ!

Are You the Christ?

Why is it easy for us to see the Divine in a young child? Well, usually, that is. When they are in their joyful, playful, and loving moments, when they are sleeping, or curling up in our laps. We also find it easier to recognize the Christ in them when they are dancing for the sheer joy of the dance.

And yet, there are times we forget. We miss that they too are the Christ when they are crying or angry or on the floor having a fabulous temper tantrum. Then, too, they are the Christ. They need to dance while the yearning to be reconnected to the Beloved is tearing them apart. Even then—when they are totally unaware of anything but the sheer despair of this moment of their life—even then, they are the Christ.

He cried out in despair in the gardens of Gethsemane. Yet, even in that moment, he was the Christ. Do you see him here, in the white tutu and ballet slippers, calling to you to remember him, to remind you what he came to teach?

Are You the Christ?

Can I see this woman, I mean, really see into the heart of her? I see her appearance as she walks, so fearful, so full of worry and despair. She folds in on herself, has given up the dreams of a life filled with joy, happiness, and love. She does what needs to be done. She is practiced at hiding herself in a small container to avoid detection. This is what we may see when we stop our search here on the outside: the appearance of a frightened woman with no future, no courage.

What happens if we mine deeper? If we call her outdoors under the stars and a full moon, what then might we find?

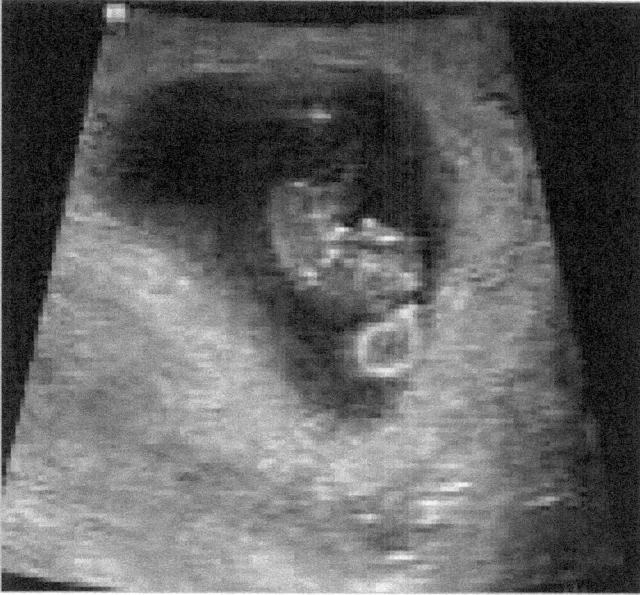

Are You the Christ?

Rather than looking at the decisions—right and wrong—that we make as humans, let us look at who we see as the Christ and who we do not see in this way.

Do we focus on the fact that there is something inside a woman, changing her chemistry, her emotions, her understanding of who she is, and who she will be forever? Or do we talk instead of the developing embryo, not yet considered a fetus? Or of the woman whose life and self are being forever altered?

She may know or guess the cause of these changes in her body, in her head, in her heart. She may know what she will choose to do about these new changes. Or she may be at a loss. At some point, a choice will be made, conscious or not. She will be forever changed and affected no matter what she chooses: to have a child to keep in her life, to love, honor, and raise to adulthood; or to carry the child for forty weeks, feel it, protect it, and then unselfishly offer it to another to complete its development; or to go no further with these changes.

These decisions again forever change the woman making them.

Are you the Christ? Are you the judge and jury? Or are you the woman with the choices to make?

TODAY

I
Do not
Want to step so quickly
Over a beautiful line on God's palm
As I move through the earth's
Marketplace
Today.

I do not want to touch any object in this world
Without my eyes testifying to the truth
That everything is
My Beloved.

Something has happened
To my understanding of existence
That now makes my heart always full of
wonder
And kindness.

I do not
Want to step so quickly
Over this sacred place on God's body
That is right beneath your
Own foot

As I
Dance with
Precious life
Today.

—Hafiz (tr. Ladinsky)

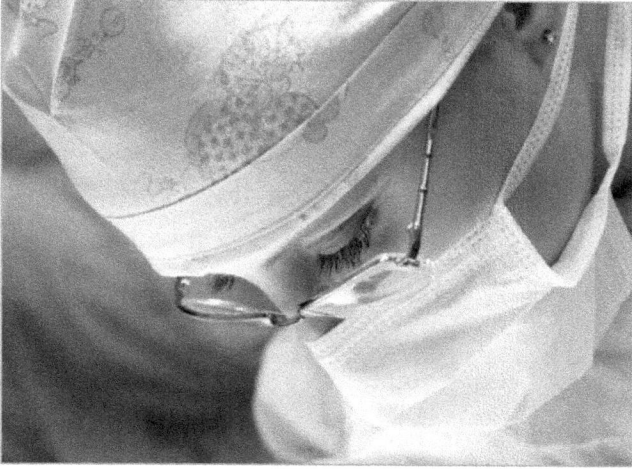

Are You the Christ?

I have walked in the world of medicine for the last three decades. So many times, I have been in the presence of wonder. So many times, I have missed the fleeting opportunity to recognize the Christ.

It seems so easy to see the Christ in this woman who is saving the lives of children. Who but a saint would do such a thing? The Christ, of course, is here in her work, saving lives, keeping families together. But as she finishes her work and heads out into the night, what does she recognize of who she is and what she has accomplished? Does she look in the mirror and see the light of the Christ smiling back at her? Does she feel overwhelmed with all there is still left to do? Can she allow herself the blessing to know that she is the Christ? That she too is working miracles, today, now, in the town of your choice?

Is she the Christ because of the clothes she wears, or where she works, or what she does? Is she the Christ because she can save a life? Does the way we see her diminish others who may do things less noble? In her shadow, how many others—whose deeds or kindnesses are less remarkable, not so extraordinary, or dramatic—do we simply dismiss? Or miss altogether?

What if, just what if everything—I mean everything in existence—does point to God? Then who might we recognize as the Christ?

Are You the Christ?

When I peer at you, I see the bad jokes from my past that surround and characterize "the lawyer." You know the ones I mean, the jokes that claim a lawyer cannot possibly get into heaven—let alone be the Christ! My rational/logical mind does not allow me to notice the Christ within you.

Are You the Christ?

As I am graced to remember to breathe and connect to that Beloved place inside myself, that place that lights up the room and brings clarity where there was only darkness, I am surprised by the recognition that, yes, you too just might be the Christ; a man in a suit, who makes money and walks with the moneychangers, a man who makes a living off the difficulties of others.

Did the Christ walk among those who were thought to be unclean, unworthy? You too may be someone who has come to light up the world, to spread light in the darkest of corners. You are the Beloved, in just another costume. You, too, may just be the Christ.

BETWEEN YOUR EYE
AND THIS PAGE

Between
Your eye and this page
I am standing.

Between
Your ear and sound
The Friend has pitched a golden tent
Your spirit walks through a thousand times
A day.

Each time you pass the Kaaba
The Sun unwinds a silk thread from your body.
Each time you pass any object
From within it
I bow.

If you are still having doubts
About His nearness

Once in a while debate with God.

Between
Your eye and this page Hafiz
Is standing.

Bump
Into me
More.

—*Hafiz (tr. Ladinsky)*

Are You the Christ?

We wander the world, sometimes looking into the eyes of others, sometimes looking through them, as if the person is not there. Today, I took a moment—just a moment—to look into the eyes of this young man. I took the time to stop and truly peer into their depths. Yes, he appears different than those in my family or the group of people I call friends. Does that change who he is, what he is here to do for me and all those others whose lives he touches?

Today, I took the time to ask myself, that place of inner wisdom, as I looked into his eyes, are You the Christ? Even though the way you dress, your stance, and your attitude make me uncomfortable, can you be that still? When the Christ walked this earth and others looked upon him, did they too feel a sensation of discomfort? Did he, too, stir up similar feelings and questions of "Who are you?" and "Why are you a part of my life?"

You have the appearance of a prisoner. Truthfully though, that could be either of us: you, a prisoner in your physical form in this moment caught in a photograph, but me a prisoner in my heart and mind. But in this moment—in each and every moment I live— each and every person I encounter has the opportunity to open my heart to Truth. Which of us is truly the prisoner? One of us, both of us, or perhaps I am the only prisoner here. How do I close myself to the recognition that you too are the Christ? You too are the light of God. You too are the Beloved.

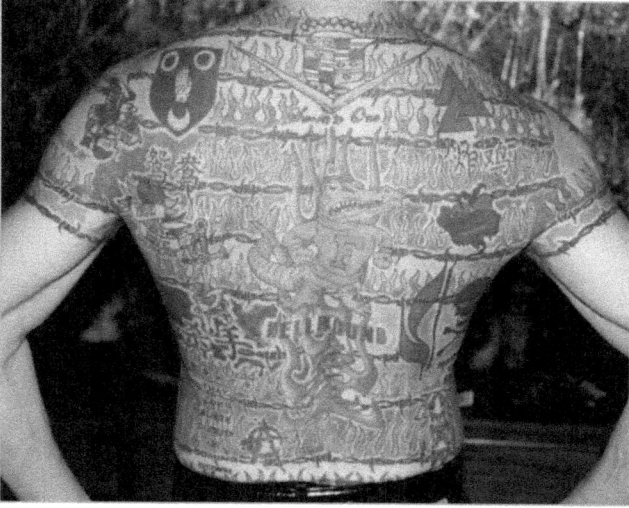

Are You the Christ?

I see you. What I mean is, I really cannot help but look at you. Everywhere I look, I see color, peeking out from under the hem of your pants, up and down your arms, your legs, across your back, all the way up your neck, even around your face. And I see the sign of the pain you had to endure to allow them to consume your body—your facial expressions, your stance, the way you wear your clothing. Hell, yes, you can believe I see and notice you.

But how do I see you? How do I feel inside as I look at you? As my stomach contracts with anxiety, my heart pounds, and my breathing speeds, I can tell you that my reaction has nothing to do with excitement and joy. It is a fight or flight response. Fear.

Why do I tremble, not with anticipation but with anxiety? Aren't you another face of the Christ? Is this another opportunity to recognize and honor that spark of the Beloved in each of us? If I stop, wait, and take the time to look deeply into your eyes, your very soul, what then will I find? Someone to be afraid of? Or will I find the person I have spent my whole life searching for? Searching high and low, hoping upon hope to be shown the truth of who I am.

As I walk beside you, you open the door to my heart where I know the Christ resides within me. Yes, you truly are the Christ, one of many who can undo the locks I have placed on my heart.

HOW DO I LISTEN?

How

Do I

Listen to others?

As if everyone were my Master

Speaking to me

His

Cherished

Last

Words.

—Hafiz (tr. Ladinsky)

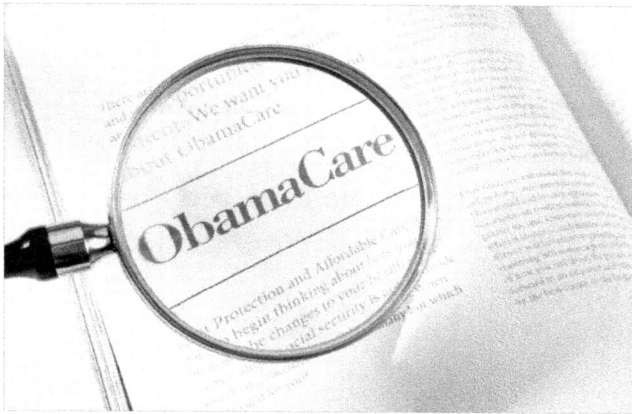

Are You the Christ?

As I sit here and look at this photograph, multiple things cross my mind. Oh yes, to me, he surely embodies the Christ, that one is easy; he appears to want to help others. He seems cool, calm, and collected under fire. He is willing to put his regular life on hold to help a nation. He simply has the appearance of calm.

Now that's me. What do you see?

Do you see someone lying to the people, someone telling lies to all who listen? Do you only see someone trying to bully people into doing things his way, without regard for what is best for the country? Someone trying to bankrupt the nation steal your money, your freedom, and your guns.

Hmm. Are we both correct, or neither? What if he is the Christ? Will you invite him to your table?

Are You the Christ?

Who are these people? They cover their faces and their heads; they cover themselves from head to toe. What are they hiding? Their faces are concealed by beards. Their eyes appear shielded.

What do I see or hear when I look at them? Towers falling, planes crashing, cars and people exploding? Death, destruction, and judgment scream though my head. Simply getting on a plane or a bus, there they are. Or rather, there they might be?

Is this someone I need to fear? Or could this be someone who prays to Allah multiple times a day? Someone who holds all of creation in awe? Could you be someone who looks into my eyes with compassion and understanding? I am not sure who you might be. And here again, Beloved, "You arrive as a cruel action wearing a guise, tricking me into thinking it is someone other than you."

Are You the Christ?

I notice you on the corner at night, or maybe during the daylight hours. Not the best corner or the safest corner, but there you are. It is cold and dark. Your clothes are cheap and there are not enough of them to keep you warm.

Are You the Christ?

A car pulls up and you quickly put on the smile, the attitude. You beg to whomever might listen that this be the last tonight. I wonder if you worry, on the one hand, about your own safety but then, on the other, display your walk, tight skirt, and pretend smile.

Whom I see now and later has nothing to do with you, but all to do with me and who I am in this moment. Can I see you as the Christ, even though you are walking a path I do not agree with? Even if I believe that what you do is okay, are you Holy or only a pitiful human? Are you the Christ?

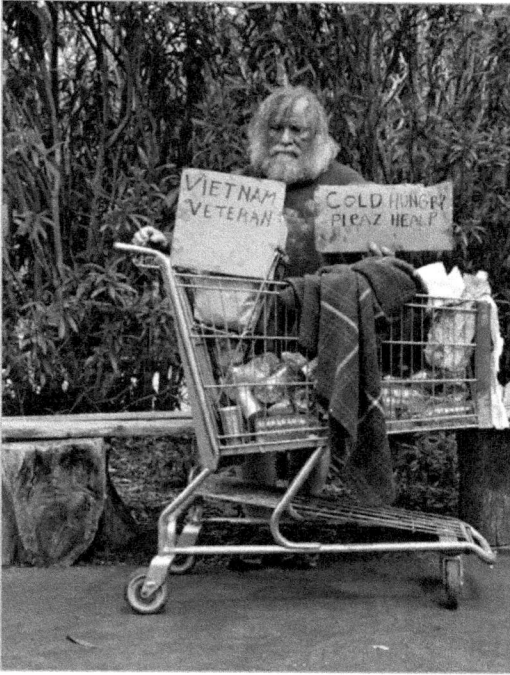

Are You the Christ?

How easy it is to ride or walk past you. All it takes is a turn of my head. Avert my eyes and you disappear to me. Maybe, just for a moment, you pull at something deep inside my chest, my heart. Maybe I feel guilty, just for an instant, because you might really be in trouble, indeed, hungry and cold, not simply trying to trick me out of something that is mine.

How often do I refuse to look at you, to allow you to pull me close? And then, and then, there are the times when I see you for who you are. I truly see another human, another face of Christ who is waiting to be noticed or recognized as who they truly are: the Christ disguised as a human being.

STAY WITH US

You
Leave
Our company when you speak
Of shame

And this makes
Everyone in the Tavern sad.

Stay with us
As we do the hardest work of rarely
Laying down
That pick and
Shovel

That will keep
Revealing our deeper kinship
With
God,

That will keep revealing
Our own divine
Worth.

You leave the company of the Beloved's friends
Whenever you speak of
Guilt,

And this makes
Everyone in the tavern
Very sad.

Stay with us tonight
As we weave love

And reveal ourselves,
Reveal ourselves

As His precious
Garments.

—Hafiz (tr. Ladinsky)

Are You the Christ?

As I look at you, as I am able to peer deep into your eyes, I can see their fiery depths, along with the depth and darkness of the void, as I squint among the shadows. I hear your words and learn your teachings, and when I stop holding my breath and huddling in on myself, I can open to the possibilities of the future—one of light reflecting off the canvas of life, one in which I place my heart and soul into the very depths of each day.

Now, that is me. That is what I get to see when I look at you, the Christ light shining.

What do others see? They may get stuck on the jewelry of stones. They may wonder what you mean when you speak of our divinity, power, truth, wholeness, and balance using whole brain integration and subtle energies. You are asking us to embody spirit on earth using the language of energy. Can they see a person with knowledge and wisdom? Will their fear of displacement or hell cause them to sin or miss the mark as they look into your eyes? Will they worry over what others may say if they see your truth? Will their teachings cause them to deny what they feel to be true in their hearts?

Well, for me, in this moment, yes, you are the Christ, and I am blessed to recognize that.

Are You the Christ?

Who are you today, this instant? Who do you think you are? Who are you pretending to be? Do you know yourself? Are things so jumbled up and moving so fast, you are not sure yourself? So you just put on that outfit, that face, that attitude.

I know what I see: a person so full of fear and uncertainty that they cannot recognize or feel the shining light. At least, in this moment, that is how you appear. Tomorrow, you are just a sullen teenager to me, pushing me to my limits. But, if I take the time, I get a glimpse of someone who wants to be pulled close and shown that the universe is a safe place to be.

I see you, you the Christ, hiding behind this tough, angry façade. You are the Christ. Do you know that? Can you feel that? Are you willing to be that?

Are You the Christ?

I believe you are. I remember the night you held that man at gunpoint to keep him from killing his wife and child. The stories talked of the day you drove wildly to get to the scene of a child's abduction, putting your life in danger to save someone you had never met. Do you remember the day you threw yourself in front of a knife to protect the old lady from that kid trying to steal her purse? Oh, yes. I believe you are. The gunman, knife man, or the woman trying to steal the child—they may have a different view. You are evil to them. You are a thorn in their sides. How about you? What do you think of yourself? Are you the Christ? Do you hold yourself up or drag yourself down? Do you consider yourself the shadow or the light?

ONLY ONE RULE

The sky
Is a suspended blue ocean.
The stars are the fish that swim.

The planets are the white whales I sometimes
Hitch a ride
On,

And the sun and all light
Have forever fused themselves into my heart
And upon my
Skin.

There is only one rule on this Wild Playground,

Every sign Hafiz has ever seen
Reads the same.

They all say,

"Have fun, my dear; my dear, have fun,
In the Beloved's divine
Game,

O, in the Beloved's
Wonderful
Game."

—*Hafiz (tr. Ladinsky*

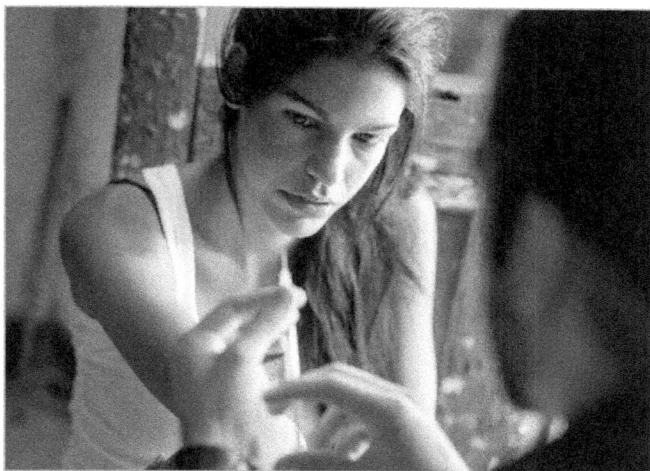

Are You the Christ?

You slip right by me; you stand beside me in a store and take my money. Or you care for my injured child in the hospital. Or you may even sleep beside me at night. I don't notice your pain and longing, and your wish to be free of your demons.

How have I missed all the signs? Is it because you don't look like my idea of a drug addict? Is it because I want to believe the best in you?

Are You the Christ?

How will I hold you when you steal my precious things to sell for your hunger, your emptiness? How will I look upon you when you are selling, not only my things, but your body and soul to fill that hole that is eating you alive? Will I see the Christ or a thief? Maybe neither. Maybe both.

Are You the Christ?

I try not to look. When I say look, I mean stare, but how do I not? You are so large, take up so much space. You look so . . . uncomfortable. Or is it me who is uncomfortable, knowing that I will need to sit beside you on the train or in the movie, knowing your size will invade my smaller space?

I wonder to myself, how did this happen? How did you let yourself get to these proportions? Do you have no control? But wait.

Who is it without control? Was it me who ate all those cookies last night? Was it me who went speeding through the red light? Was it me who continued to drink past the point of being able to stand?

Does our lack of control change who you and I truly are? Does the fact that we seem unable to control our cravings, that we fill our inner needs with things that bring disease and discomfort rather than things that bring us health and happiness, does this change the fact that we too are the Christ, that we too can give and receive a love that is unsurpassed by all things physical? If I allow myself to sit close, to sit with my discomfort that this too could easily be me, to really stop, look, and embrace my feelings, I see that you too are the Christ.

NOW IS THE TIME

Now is the time to know
That all that you do is sacred.

Now, why not consider
A lasting truce with yourself and God.

Now is the time to understand
That all your ideas of right and wrong
Were just a child's training wheels
To be laid aside
When you can finally live
With veracity
And love.

Hafiz is a divine envoy
Whom the Beloved
Has written a holy message upon.

My dear, please tell me,
Why do you still
Throw sticks at your heart
And God?

What is it in that sweet voice inside
That incites you to fear?

Now is the time for the world to know
That every thought and action is sacred.

This is the time
For you to deeply compute the impossibility

That there is anything
But Grace.

Now is the season to know
That everything you do
Is sacred.

—Hafiz (tr. Ladinsky)

Are You the Christ?

I cast around to make sure no one catches me secretly watching you. I am intrigued with your ability to prance around dressed as someone other than whom WE think you are, proudly displaying the feathers and lace, or the wife beaters and a short, short haircut.

First, we see the clothes, the accessories, the hair. Then we judge. But the issue here is not what we see. The issue is not even you. It is the WE who have decided you must be what WE think you are, the girl's or the boy's body you were born into. Certainly, you should not be other than who WE think you are.

Does it matter that you are tormented every minute of every day? Does it matter that you would never have picked this path of separation to walk, if you had a choice? No, certainly not. You need to take off those clothes and put on the disguise like the rest of us.

Hmmm, I wonder what was said about the Christ? Did he wear the right clothing? Did he follow the expected rules that THEY felt were Godly? Did he fit the mold? Am I willing to see him in your eyes?

Are You the Christ?

I I watch your struggle as you move from place to place in your rolling world. I watch you maneuver the turns and doorways, and yet I still miss who and what you are. Oh, yes, you get labeled: heroic, pitiful, amazing. Or you get ignored completely. Do those labels change a single thing about you? I feel something inside that makes me wonder how you continue.

Why do you continue?

Then I stop and wonder, would I be willing to do the same in a body that won't do what I ask it to do? Do I think of you differently than others who are able to move around on their own two feet? Do I treat you as if your knowledge and understanding are as limited as your ability to move your body? Could the Christ really be traveling around in a wheelchair?

Tell me, would you? Are you the Christ?

YOU'RE IT

God
Disguised
As a myriad of things and
Playing a game
Of tag

Has kissed you and said,
"You're it—

I mean, you're Really IT!"

Now
It does not matter
What you believe or feel

For something wonderful,

Major-league Wonderful
Is someday going
To

Happen.

—Hafiz (tr. Ladinsky)

Are You the Christ?

You sit on the bench watching the children play. So many people walk past without even looking in your direction, as if you are part of the bench itself. No one looks or speaks as you search in their eyes for recognition, recognition that you still exist, as you sit here waiting, recognition that you breathe and speak and have so much wisdom to share.

Are You the Christ?

Are you the reservoir for the secrets of the ages past, or will you just talk in circles?

You are unable to work and be "productive" like the rest of us. Do you wonder yourself what you have left to offer to a world that honors only youth, beauty, and strength?

As I slow down and take the time to sit beside you, look deeply into your eyes, no words need even be spoken. In that instant of connection of presence, it is obvious that, yes, you are the Christ.

Are You the Christ?

When you pull up beside me, I look at you out of the corner of my eye. Your motorcycle is loud, and your face to me is fearful. You look at me and smile, eyes crinkling against the sun, teeth flashing. What are you smiling about? My discomfort? The frightened look on my face as you continue to stare?

What if, just what if, your thoughts are on love and peace and the joy of the wind in your hair? What if you are thinking about how wonderful it feels to have your hand on the thigh of your wife sitting behind you? Could you be thinking about holding your first grandchild?

What if, just what if, you are wearing a smile because you know, you know that, not only are you the Christ, but as you drove by me at eighty miles per hour, you too were blessed with looking deeply into the eyes of the Christ.

ALL THE TALENTS OF GOD

All the talents of God are within you.

How could this be otherwise
When your soul
Derived from His
Genes!

I love that expression,
"All the talents of God are within you."

Sometimes Hafiz cannot help but to applaud
Certain words that rise from my depths

Like the scent of a lover's
Body.

Hold this book close to your heart
For it contains wonderful
Secrets.

—*Hafiz (tr. Ladinsky)*

Are You the Christ?

We have walked our life together for twenty-six years. There have been days when I could not see the Christ in you even if you had grown a beard, worn sandals, and a long white robe, even if the world around you followed you and you walked on water. Why is that? Why don't I recognize that place of holiness within the person who is closest to me? What is it about being so close to someone that we color them with our own set of markers?

You walked five hundred miles across Spain, following the trail of St. James. You walked that path so many thousands have walked before us, to assure my safety, even though, at the time, I did not believe I needed your protection. Not knowing that you would find that experience of the Christ, you offered your strength and time to follow a way that I hoped would bring us closer to recognizing the Presence in all of those around us.

I am graced to have walked this path where you were transformed, transformed in my eyes even now, in our day to day routine. I am gifted to see you more often as you truly are: a man, who loves and cares passionately for all those he meets, related by blood or not; a man who protects me and our family even when we do not recognize the need; a man who gives of himself untiringly.

Are You the Christ?

Is this the reason we live with and around others, so that we have the opportunity to grow and see the TRUTH of who they are?

I could not have walked the Trail to Santiago without you, and now each day, I get to see the light of Christ shine within my own home.

Are You the Christ?

This will tell the truth of whether I have actually changed after my pilgrimage and can truly see the Christ in one who betrayed me deeply. One who helped shape my childhood, teenage years, and up into my late twenties, in ways that left a wreckage of misplaced love. *Tear Stains on My Pillow, A Woman's Journey to*

Freedom was born because of you, a man who taught me things no child should be taught. How to use their bodies to find love and affection, how to keep a secret that cannot be shared, to turn an innocent young girl into something shameful and unlovable. This is what you gave me. Even as I trusted and loved you, you twisted my young understanding of what must be done to be loved.

This changed who I was for a very long time, lay hidden in my psyche until I was in my forties, when, surprisingly, my mind opened and allowed me to see what I had experienced. So many things became clear—the way I had lived my life, the things I had done that still, to this day, I have never spoken about to anyone.

What do I see now as I look at you? Can I see a man who had no idea what he was causing? Maybe a man who had experienced the same type of treatment as a youngster himself. I will never know the answers to these questions and many others, because you are no longer around for me to ask. Yet, at this moment, I can look, and remember you and your gentle side, your playful and caring sides, the smile of the Christ that I saw when I was that innocent child.

Today, I am willing to see what is true within you. Yes, you too are the Christ.

WHAT IS THE ROOT?

What

Is the

Root of all these

Words?

One thing: love.

But a love so deep and sweet

It needed to express itself

With scents, sounds, colors

That never before

Existed.

—*Hafiz (tr. Ladinsky)*

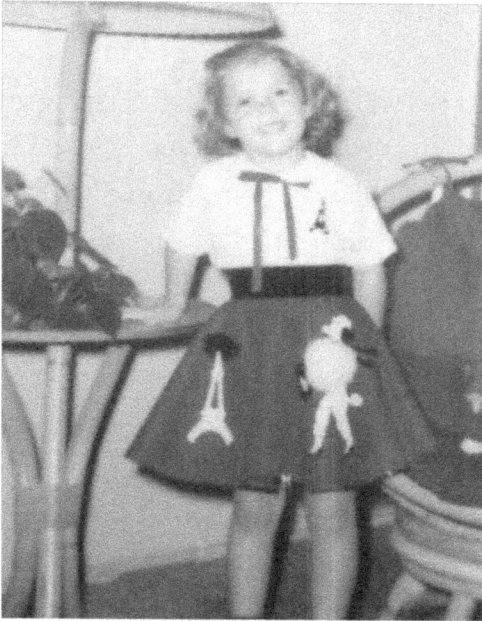

Are You the Christ?

So it appears this book will end with me, the one this book decided to come through. Is it wisdom or lunacy? I guess each of us will have to decide for ourselves. There are days I look at this picture, or more likely look at myself in the mirror, and wonder, who is that staring out at me? Who is this woman, and what does she want?

I have watched this child/girl grow into adulthood, and I have lived the sometimes guilt-ridden days when I could not see her Truth. And then, and then, there are the moments of absolute clarity, of absolute knowing that I too am Holy, I too am the Christ.

This knowing is an exquisite gift, even if only for a fleeting moment, on a sunny day—a gift so grand that I offer the same opportunity to you. Allow the person who sneaks up on you as you pass a store window—you know the one—allow yourself to be known for your truth, for your innate holiness and ability to guide yourself so that you too may recognize the many faces of the Christ that walk past you each day.

The Truth is YOU ARE THE CHRIST. You too have that Christ being within you. I would love to believe that this book will open your heart and your mind to the infinite possibility of the Christ presence in your life and to know that this includes you.

THE GUEST HOUSE

This being human is a guest house.
Every morning a new arrival.
A joy, a depression, a meanness,
some momentary awareness comes
as an unexpected visitor.
Welcome and entertain them all!
Even if they are a crowd of sorrows,
who violently sweep your house
empty of its furniture,
still, treat each guest honorably.
He may be clearing you out
for some new delight.
The dark thought, the shame, the malice.
meet them at the door laughing and
invite them in.
Be grateful for whatever comes.
because each has been sent
as a guide from beyond.

—Jelaluddin Rumi,
translation by Coleman Barks

About the Author

K. Morgan deCasenave Patterson

has spent her life wanting to walk closely with God. As a young child who was not raised with any religious training, she took herself into the Catholic Church near her home. There she sat through Latin masses and received communion, knowing that something deep and powerful was calling to her. At the age of twenty, she was introduced to meditation by an Indian Guru and she still practices this form to this day.

She is open to experiencing God from many differing perspectives and has taught Mindfulness meditation to high school students and women in prison. She has explored the Native American-based practices, including Vision Quest, Sweat Lodges, Pipe Ceremony, and Drumming. The last twenty years, she has added the teachings of Unity Church to her practices and served on the board of directors of Unity Eastside Church in Tallahassee, Florida.

In 2014, Morgan and her husband walked the Camino de Santiago in Spain, a five hundred-mile trail also known as the Way of Saint James. Making that journey was a longtime desire of hers. Before she left, this book, *Are You the Christ*, was mostly completed. It came as an idea and essentially wrote itself. After coming home, Morgan realized that the last three stories were not only needed but ready and willing to be told. So in the summer of 2015, the book was completed and ready to share. We hope it stirs up your everyday life and opens you to a whole new way of viewing humanity!